Silly Sketcher

Draw Funny Holiday Pictures!

written by Luke Colins

illustrated by Catherine Cates

BLACK
RABBIT
BOOKS

Hi Jinx is published by Black Rabbit Books
P.O. Box 3263, Mankato, Minnesota, 56002.
www.blackrabbitbooks.com
Copyright © 2020 Black Rabbit Books

Jennifer Besel, editor; Catherine Cates,
interior designer; Michael Sellner, cover designer;
Omay Ayres, photo researcher

Library of Congress Cataloging-in-Publication Data
Names: Colins, Luke, author.
Title: Draw funny holiday pictures! / by Luke Colins.
Description: Mankato, Minnesota : Black Rabbit Books, 2020. |
Series: Hi jinx. Silly sketcher | Includes bibliographical references and
index. | Audience: Ages 8-12. | Audience: Grades 4 to 6.
Identifiers: LCCN 2018018967 | ISBN 9781680729498 (library binding) |
ISBN 9781680729559 (ebook) | ISBN 9781644660744 (paperback)
Subjects: LCSH: Cartooning—Technique—Juvenile literature. |
Holidays in art—Juvenile literature.
Classification: LCC NC1764 .C6535 2020 |
DDC 741.5/1—dc23
LC record available at https://lccn.loc.gov/2018018967

Printed in China. 1/19

Image Credits

Alamy: Matthew Cole, 5; iStock: carbouval, 5; Shutterstock: anfisa focusova,
19; Mario Pantelic, Cover, Back Cover, 3, 5, 12; Memo Angeles, Cover, 4,
5, 6, 9, 10, 10–11, 13, 16, 18, 20, 23; NastyaBob, 20; Olga Sabo, 2–3, 5;
opicobello, 6, 15, 17; owatta, 5; Pasko Maksim, Back Cover, 11, 23, 24; Pitju,
3, 9, 21; Ron Dale, Cover, 1, 3, 4, 5, 6, 7, 11, 15, 20; Sudowoodo, 20; Tueris,
10; world of vector, 20 Every effort has been made to contact copyright
holders for material reproduced in this book. Any omissions will be
rectified in subsequent printings if notice is given to the publisher.

Contents

CHAPTER 1

Be a Silly Sketcher! 4

CHAPTER 2

Put Your Pencil to
the Paper. 6

CHAPTER 3

Get in on the Hi Jinx. .20

Other Resources. 22

Chapter 1
Be a Silly Sketcher!

Holidays are fun times (except when Grandma pinches your cheek). Make your holidays even better with some art. Sketch up something silly to celebrate.

To be a silly sketcher, all you need is a pencil, some paper, and a funny bone. Draw a circle here. Add squiggles there. Just follow the steps. You'll have hilarious holiday art in no time.

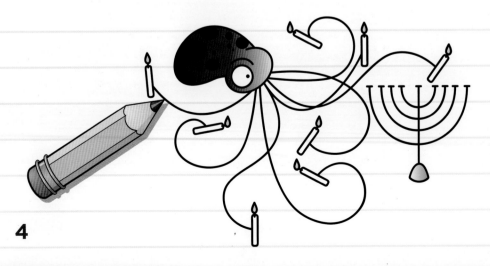

What You Need

pencils

pencil sharpener
(just in case)

lots of paper   eraser

colored pencils and markers

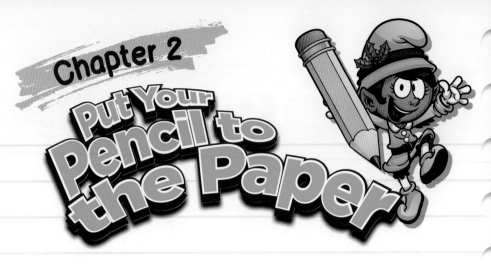

Chapter 2
Put Your Pencil to the Paper

Let's start with a simple sketch to get the giggles going. Draw a laughing Christmas tree, and feel free to chuckle along!

Step 1
Use a curved line to make a Christmas tree shape.

Step 2
Give the tree a silly face.

Step 3

Add a trunk and some arm branches. Top the tree with a star.

Step 4

Use circles for **ornaments**.

Step 5

Add **motion** lines to show your tree shaking with laughter.

Finish It Up!

Use markers to **outline** your drawing. Then try colored pencils for shading it in.

Lucky Clover

Stories say a four-leaf clover is good luck. Bring good luck to your St. Patrick's Day with this silly sketch.

Step 1
Draw four connected heart shapes to start the clover.

Step 2
Add big circle eyes and a little hat.

Step 3
Erase the lines inside the **overlapping** shapes.

Step 4

Add details to the eyes and hat. Draw on a mouth too.

Step 5

Give the clover funny arms and legs.

Step 6

Sketch in motion lines to make your clover jump.

Roll-Away Pumpkin

Draw this funny pumpkin for some silly Halloween fun.

Step 1

Use ovals and half ovals to make the pumpkin shape.

Step 2

Give the pumpkin a stem. Add motion lines to show that it's rolling away.

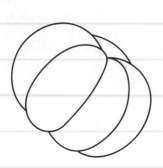

Step 3

Erase the lines inside the overlapping shapes.

Step 4

Add big circle eyes. Offset the **pupils** for a dizzy look.

Step 5

Don't forget the eyebrows and a mouth.

Olive You!

Olives aren't usually Valentine's Day characters. But when you make them a **pun**, your valentine will giggle with love.

Step 1

Draw two ovals on your paper. Then add two big circles on top of each oval.

Step 2

Add smaller ovals inside the big ovals. Draw a decorative heart too.

Step 3

Erase the lines inside the overlapping shapes.

 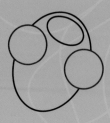

Step 4
Use curved lines and dots to give the characters arms and legs.

Step 5
Finish the faces with pupils and mouths. Add some detail hearts too.

OLIVE YOU, VALENTINE!

Step 6
Draw motion lines around the characters. Add a silly phrase too.

OLIVE YOU, VALENTINE!

The Hanukkah Octopus

Eight arms would be perfect for lighting eight Hanukkah candles. Right?

Step 1

Draw a half circle. Give the bottom line a little curve. Add an oval on top of the right side of the half circle.

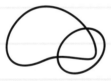

Step 2

Erase the lines inside the overlapping shapes.

Step 3

Give the octopus eight squiggly arms. They can crisscross or curve. It's up to you!

Tip

Make sure to draw the arms spread out.
Then you'll have room for all the candles.

Step 4

Add a big circle eye
and details.

Step 5

Draw a rectangle at the
end of each arm. Use
straight and curved lines
to draw the menorah.

Step 6

Give each candle a flame.
Add details to the
menorah too.

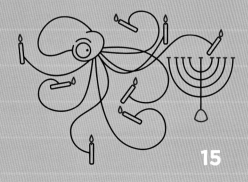

Turkey Trot

Thanksgiving is a tricky situation for any turkey. Draw this bird trying to run away.

Step 1
Use curved lines to start the turkey's body, wings, and eyes.

Step 2
Add the bird's beak and **wattle**. Start its legs too.

Step 3
Erase the lines inside the overlapping shapes.

Step 4
Use long ovals to give your turkey feathers.

Step 5

Erase the lines inside the overlapping shapes.

Step 6

Add pupils. Finish the legs and wings.

Step 7

Draw a curved detail line on the chest. Put in motion lines too.

Finish It Up!

Draw a dining room table for your turkey to run on!

Hippity Hop

The Easter Bunny brings candy. Your Easter Bunny sketch will be just as sweet.

Step 1

Start the body with a long oval. Add a **lopsided** circle head and oval ears.

Step 2

Add eyes, legs, and a fluffy tail.

Step 3

Erase the lines inside the
overlapping shapes.

Step 4

Give the bunny a mouth
holding a basket.

Step 5

Erase the lines inside the
overlapping shapes.

Step 6

Add pupils to the eyes.
Put eggs in the basket.
A few eggs can fly out too.

Step 7

Add motion lines to show
the bunny hopping.

Chapter 3
Get in on the Hi Jinx

Graphic artists use the same steps you just did! They use simple shapes to build the frames of their drawings. Then they add details, such as shading and color. Their holiday drawings are sometimes used on greeting cards. Maybe someday you'll make great holiday cards!

HAPPY HALLOWEEN

Take It One Step More

1. Most of the drawings tell you to erase the lines inside overlapping shapes. Why should you do that?

2. Are your sketches more or less funny with color? Why?

3. What features make these drawings funny?

GLOSSARY

lopsided (LAHP-sy-did)—uneven on one side

motion (MO-shun)—an act or process of moving

ornament (OR-nuh-muhnt)—small objects put on something else to make it more attractive

outline (AHWT-lyn)—to draw a line around the edges of something

overlap (oh-vur-LAP)—to extend over or past

pun (PUHN)—a joke that plays with words that sound similar or with different meanings of a word or phrase

pupil (PYU-pul)—the part of the eye that lets light in; in people, it's the round, black part of the eye.

trace (TRAYS)—to copy something by following the lines or letters as seen through a transparent sheet on top

wattle (WAH-tuhl)—a fleshy part usually around the head or neck of a bird

BOOKS

Johnson, Clare. *How to Draw.* New York: Dorling Kindersley Limited, 2017.

Let's Draw Animals with Crayola! Crayola. Minneapolis: Lerner Publications, 2018.

Nguyen, Angela. *How to Draw Cute Stuff: Draw Anything and Everything in the Cutest Style Ever!* New York: Sterling Children's Books, 2017.

WEBSITES

Drawing for Kids
mocomi.com/fun/arts-crafts/drawing-for-kids/

How to Draw
www.hellokids.com/r_12/drawing-for-kids/

How to Draw Archive
**www.artforkidshub.com/
how-to-draw/**

TIPS AND TRICKS

Make sure to let the marker outlines dry before coloring in your drawings.

Colored pencils are a great tool for coloring in your drawings. Layer a color over another for a cool blended effect.

Can't draw a straight line? Try using a ruler or other straight edge.

Don't worry if your drawings don't look exactly like the ones in this book! Art is all about creating your own thing. Just have fun!